Keep Yourself Safe on the Internet

Passwords Are Secret

Anthony Ardely

PowerKiDS press.

NEW YORK

Published in 2018 by The Rosen Publishing Group, Inc.
29 East 21st Street, New York, NY 10010

Editor: Greg Roza
Book Design: Rachel Rising
Interior Layout: Michael Flynn

Photo Credits: Cover JGI/Tom Grill/Blend Images/Getty Images; cover, pp. 3–4, 6, 8, 10, 12, 14, 16, 18, 20, 22–24 (background) Creative Mood/
Shutterstock.com; p. 5 Â© Corbis/Corbis/Getty Images; p. 7 24Novembers/Shutterstock.com; p. 9 VectorWeb/Shutterstock.com; p. 11 Dragon
Images/Shutterstock.com; p. 13 PeopleImages/E+/Getty Images; p. 15 KK Tan/Shutterstock.com; p. 17 Ruslan Guzov/Shutterstock.com;
p. 19 Monkey Business Images/Shutterstock.com; p. 21 Vertigo3d/E+/Getty Images; p. 22 FlashMovie/Shutterstock.com.

Cataloging-in-Publication Data

Names: Ardely, Anthony.
Title: Passwords are secret / Anthony Ardely.
Description: New York : PowerKids Press, 2018. | Series: Keep yourself safe on the internet | Includes index.
Identifiers: ISBN 9781508162988 (pbk.) | ISBN 9781538325094 (library bound) | ISBN 9781538325810 (6 pack)
Subjects: LCSH: Computers--Access control--Passwords--Juvenile literature. | Internet--Security measures--Juvenile literature.
Classification: LCC QA76.9.A25 A73 2018 | DDC 005.8--dc23

Manufactured in China

CPSIA Compliance Information: Batch #BW18PK For further information contact Rosen Publishing, New York, New York at 1-800-237-9932.

Contents

Secret Passwords

It's fun to go online. You can talk to friends, play games, listen to music, and learn new things. Whatever you do, always be safe online!

5

Some **websites** might ask you to make up a **password**. A password is a secret word you **create**. Passwords are for your own safety.

Your password should be easy for you to remember and hard for others to guess. Passwords can have both uppercase and lowercase letters. They can also have numbers.

MEMBER LOG IN

SallySmith

LOGIN

MEMBER LOG IN

sAllY_sMith

LOGIN

BEST PASSWORD

MEMBER LOG IN

3A11y_3th

LOGIN

Passwords Are Private

Your passwords are **private**. It's not safe to share them with other people, even your friends. However, always share passwords with your parents.

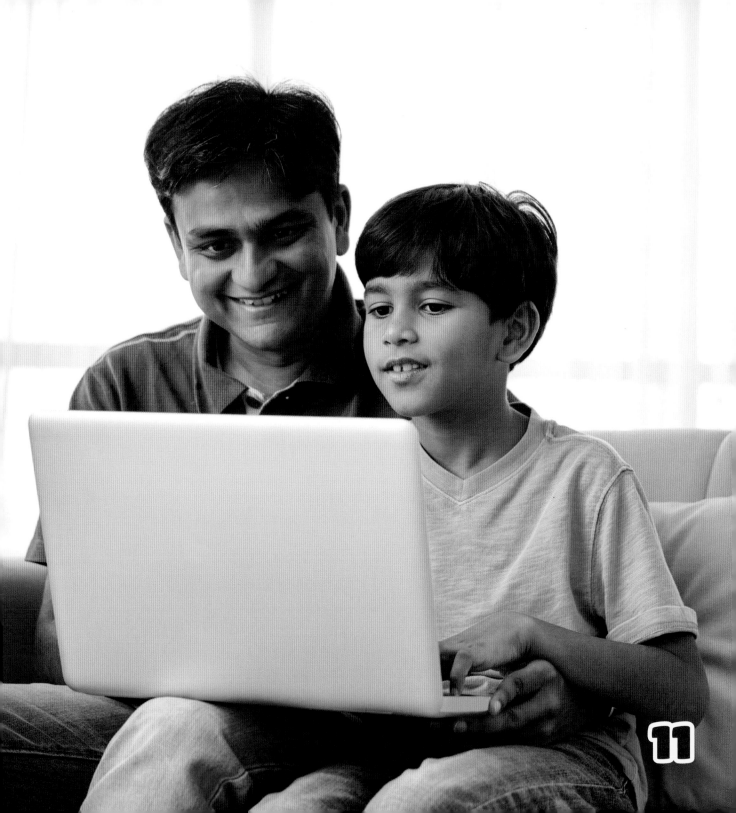

11

Many websites require a password. Don't use the same password all the time. Try to remember your passwords rather than writing them down where someone could see them.

Stolen Passwords

Someone could **steal** your password if it's easy to guess. Don't use your birthday or other things people know about you for your password.

A stranger is someone you don't know. Strangers could use your password to see private facts about you. These facts are unsafe for strangers to know.

Tell a parent or teacher if your password is stolen. Tell them as soon as you know. They will help you.

An adult can help you make a new password. Don't share your new password with anyone else. It should be very different from your old password.

There are many ways to stay safe on the Internet. Always keep your passwords secret. That way, you can have fun and be safe online!

Password

••••••••••••••

Login

Forgot your password?

Glossary

create: To make something.

password: A secret group of letters and numbers that lets you use some websites.

private: Not meant for other people to know.

steal: To take something in a way that is wrong.

website: A page on the Internet.

Index

Websites

Due to the changing nature of Internet links, PowerKids Press has developed an online list of websites related to the subject of this book. This site is updated regularly. Please use this link to access the list: www.powerkidslinks.com/kysi/pass